Mysterious You

Squirt!

The most interesting book you'll ever read about blood

Written by Trudee Romanek

Illustrated by Rose Cowles

Kids Can Press

To the Scott family, especially Thomas.
Thank you for sharing your story. — T.R.

My sincere thanks to two experts who took time from their very busy schedules to read through this manuscript: Dr. Bruce McManus, Professor, iCAPTURE Centre, University of British Columbia / Providence Health Care, and Director of the Centre's Cardiovascular Research Laboratory; and John Miller, MDPhD, Senior Medical Director, American Red Cross, St. Paul, Minnesota. Your contributions were extremely helpful.

A special thank you to Dr. Joel A. Kirsh, Staff Physician, Cardiology and Critical Care, The Hospital for Sick Children, Toronto, for his time and expertise. As well, I'm grateful to the following people for their assistance: Dr. Christine Boutin, Cardiologist, Hôpital Ste-Justine, Montreal; Dr. Gary L. Bowlin, Director, Tissue Engineering Laboratory, Virginia Commonwealth University; Elizabeth Brumfiel, Professor of Anthropology, Northwestern University, Evanston, Illinois; Janna Lenz and Christine Pearson, American Red Cross; Joyce Poole, International Blood Group Reference Laboratory, United Kingdom; Dennis Provencher and the Blood Donor Clinic, Camp Lester, Okinawa, Japan; and Dr. Dan Toews, Professor of Biology, Acadia University, Wolfville, Nova Scotia.

On the publishing side of things, my thanks to Kids Can for the opportunity they've given me with this series. And to Liz, Marie and Rose, you are the best kind of professionals — talented, uncompromising and fun!

Kids Can Press acknowledges the financial support of the Government of Ontario, through the Ontario Media Development Corporation's Ontario Book Initiative; the Ontario Arts Council; the Canada Council for the Arts; and the Government of Canada, through the BPIDP, for our publishing activity.

Published in Canada by
Kids Can Press Ltd.
29 Birch Avenue
Toronto, ON M4V 1E2

Published in the U.S. by
Kids Can Press Ltd.
2250 Military Road
Tonawanda, NY 14150

www.kidscanpress.com

Edited by Elizabeth MacLeod
Designed by Marie Bartholomew
Printed and bound in China

The hardcover edition of this book is smyth sewn casebound.
The paperback edition of this book is limp sewn with a drawn-on cover.

CM 06 0 9 8 7 6 5 4 3 2 1
CM PA 06 0 9 8 7 6 5 4 3 2 1

Library and Archives Canada Cataloguing in Publication Data

Romanek, Trudee
    Squirt! : the most interesting book you'll ever read about blood / written by Trudee Romanek ; illustrated by Rose Cowles.

(Mysterious you)
Includes index.

ISBN-13: 978-1-55337-776-4 (bound) ISBN-10: 1-55337-776-1 (bound)
ISBN-13: 978-1-55337-777-1 (pbk.) ISBN-10: 1-55337-777-X (pbk.)

1. Blood—Juvenile literature. 2. Heart—Juvenile literature.
I. Cowles, Rose, 1967- II. Title. III. Series: Mysterious you (Toronto, Ont.)

QP103.R64 2005   j612.1   C2005-904234-6

Kids Can Press is a [orus™ Entertainment company

- Over your lifetime, your heart will beat about 2.5 billion times.

- Don't get a Texas horned lizard angry or it'll squirt blood at you from its eyes. It's not just regular blood, either. Experts think this stuff contains toxins, or poisons, that irritate and burn any animal they splatter.

Big-hearted

Ever seen pictures of bodybuilders with muscles bulging everywhere? Their muscles are bigger because they get exercised, hard, every day. Any muscle will get bigger through exercise, including the heart.

Athletes — especially those who run long distances — have bigger, stronger hearts than most people. Because their bodies need more oxygen during exercise, the heart gets stronger and better at pumping that blood and the oxygen it carries. Once an athlete retires or stops training so much, her heart returns to its normal, smaller size.

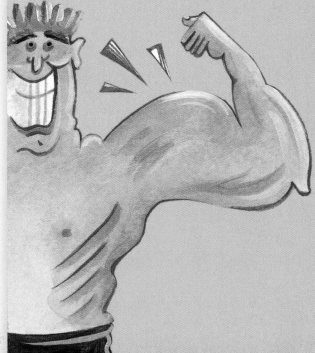

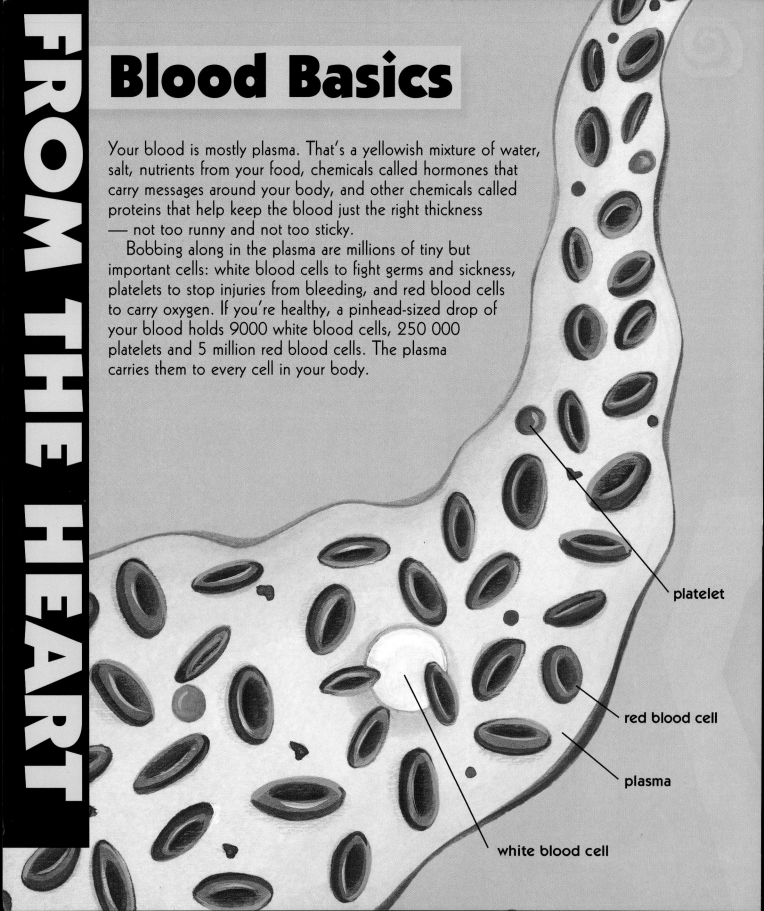

Blood Basics

Your blood is mostly plasma. That's a yellowish mixture of water, salt, nutrients from your food, chemicals called hormones that carry messages around your body, and other chemicals called proteins that help keep the blood just the right thickness — not too runny and not too sticky.

Bobbing along in the plasma are millions of tiny but important cells: white blood cells to fight germs and sickness, platelets to stop injuries from bleeding, and red blood cells to carry oxygen. If you're healthy, a pinhead-sized drop of your blood holds 9000 white blood cells, 250 000 platelets and 5 million red blood cells. The plasma carries them to every cell in your body.

platelet

red blood cell

plasma

white blood cell

Seeing Red

Your body with all its cells is like a city full of factories, stores and other businesses. Just as every business needs workers to get the work done, your many cells need oxygen to carry out their special jobs.

Red blood cells are the buses and subway trains that carry oxygen to all those cells. Part of each red blood cell is a molecule called hemoglobin (HEE-muh-globe-in). That hemoglobin contains an iron molecule, and the iron can pick up oxygen from your lungs when you breathe in. Your blood can then carry that oxygen to cells throughout your body.

Those iron molecules and the oxygen they carry are what make your red blood cells — and your blood — look red. It's kind of like how the iron in a shovel turns rusty red if it gets wet because it reacts with oxygen in the air.

The blood traveling back to your heart looks dark purply red. That's because it has dropped off its oxygen and is instead carrying carbon dioxide — a waste gas your body makes — back to your lungs so you can breathe it out.

- **The horseshoe crab's blood is blue, not red. That's because it contains copper instead of iron to pick up oxygen.**

Faulty Blood

You'd never know that Pete Sampras, seven-time Wimbledon tennis champion, has trouble getting enough oxygen to his cells. Sampras has a mild form of thalassemia (thal-ah-SEEM-me-uh). A person with this blood disorder has too little hemoglobin, or his hemoglobin isn't normal. So there aren't enough healthy red blood cells to carry oxygen throughout his body.

Doctors say that anyone who does not have enough red blood cells has a disorder called anemia (ann-NEE-me-uh). There are several types of anemia. For instance, someone with sickle cell anemia has hemoglobin that changes the shape of the red blood cells from round and fairly flat to long, curved and stiff. That means they can't fit through the narrowest blood vessels to get oxygen to all parts of the body.

normal cell

sickled cell

Your Body's First Aid Kit

Dr. Gary Bowlin is experimenting with a bandage you never have to pull off. It's made of incredibly thin strands of fibrinogen (fie-BRIN-oh-jin), a protein found in your blood. The fibers are so thin, it would take a thousand of them to match the width of one human hair.

Dr. Bowlin's team has developed a way to spin fibrinogen strands into a sort of mesh. One day, emergency workers may be able to slap pieces of this mesh on even the biggest wounds to stop the bleeding almost immediately. Unlike regular gauze, this fibrinogen patch can stay stuck to the wound and get absorbed by the body as it heals. That's because it's made of the same stuff your body produces to create its own natural bandages, which turn into scabs.

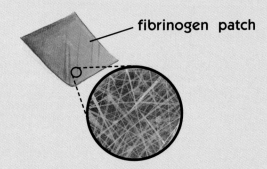

fibrinogen patch

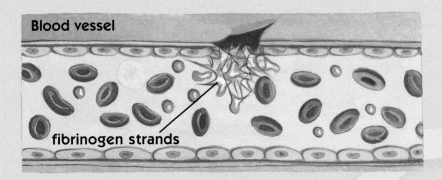

Blood vessel

fibrinogen strands

Scab Science

Your blood contains blood cells called platelets and 12 types of proteins called clotting factors. Fibrinogen is 1 of those 12. If you get a cut, fibrinogen and platelets seal you up. A chemical change in the blood that's near the cut blood vessel triggers changes in your platelets and clotting factors.

Bits of fibrinogen break off to form a mesh of fibrin (FIE-brin) strands. At the same time, the platelets get sticky and, together with the mesh forming between and around them, they plug up the hole so no more blood can leak out. As the plug of fibrin and platelets dries out, it forms a scab. It protects the injury until new skin grows over the hole.

Some people's blood is missing 1 of the 12 clotting factors. This disorder is called hemophilia (hee-moe-FEEL-ee-yuh). These people must get injections of clotting factors. Otherwise, they could bleed to death from a simple cut.

- What's a bruise? It's red blood cells that have leaked out of a broken blood vessel under your skin. When they die, they turn black. Bruises disappear as fresh blood carries off the dead cells.

You Try It

Make this model of blood to see the huge number of red blood cells it contains. You'll need yellow jelly dessert powder, 140 mL (1/2 c. plus 1 tbsp.) of red 5 mm (1/4 in.) pony beads, 50 clear seed beads and 1 white 9 mm (3/8 in.) pony bead.

1. Ask an adult to mix 20 mL (4 tsp.) of jelly powder and 80 mL (1/3 c.) boiling water in a heatproof bowl. Stir until dissolved.

2. Add 125 mL (1/2 c.) cold water. Stir, then pour into a clear bowl or glass and place in the refrigerator for one hour. Your jelly should be thick but not set.

3. Stir in the red beads. These are your red blood cells.

4. Drop in the white bead to represent a white blood cell and the clear beads to be the platelets. Stir.

Your model blood is swimming with red blood cells, just like the blood in your veins. If you weigh 36 kg (80 lb.), you have about 12 billion red blood cells.

(Pour your "blood" into a strainer and run hot water over the beads to clean them so you can reuse them.)

Not My Type

By the early 1800s, doctors had realized they could take blood from healthy people to give to ailing patients. Still, doctors couldn't figure out why some of those patients died. Then in 1901 Austrian scientist Karl Landsteiner discovered that not all human blood is the same.

Landsteiner experimented with blood from a number of people and found that some had proteins stuck to the outer layer, or membrane, of their red blood cells. There were two different kinds of these proteins, and he named them A and B.

Some people's red blood cells have both types of proteins stuck to them. Their blood type is AB. Some have just one or the other — their blood is type A or type B, depending on which protein they have. Other people's red blood cells have neither protein. These people have type O blood.

When Landsteiner mixed blood that had different proteins, the red blood cells clumped together. But if he mixed blood that had the same proteins, there was no clumping. Blood that clumps can't flow through a person's blood vessels. The mystery of the dying patients was solved. After Landsteiner's discovery, doctors realized that only certain blood could be given to certain people.

- **If your blood type is O–, you're what's called a universal donor — your blood can be given to any patient, no matter what his blood type is.**

Rh Factor

Forty years later, Landsteiner and a co-researcher noticed another protein on the red blood cells of rhesus monkeys. They called it the Rh factor, and found that many people had this protein in their blood too.

If your blood has the Rh factor, a positive symbol (+) is added after your blood type. If your blood doesn't have that protein, you are Rh negative, and a negative sign (−) is added. So, for example, you might be O+ or O−.

The Rh factor is especially important for any woman who is Rh− and is having a baby who is Rh+. When the baby is born, some of its Rh+ proteins may get mixed into the mother's bloodstream. Her blood will react by making antibodies that label the Rh+ proteins as germs to be destroyed. That won't hurt the mother, but later on, if she becomes pregnant with another baby who is Rh+, the antibodies in her blood will harm the baby growing inside her.

Rarest of the Rare

Some human blood types are more common than others. Worldwide, type O blood is the most common type.

Everyone's blood is one of the four main types — O, A, B or AB. Within those main types, though, are about 200 rare types, because some people have other, less common proteins on their red blood cells. One of those rare blood types, known as K zero, is shared by only about 60 people in the world.

Some people with very rare blood have blood taken from them when they're healthy and then have it stored in case they're injured or need surgery.

The Gift of Life

Dennis Provencher has done a lot of bleeding, but for a very good reason. On July 25, 2003, in Okinawa, Japan, Dennis donated his 231st unit of blood. Dennis began giving blood in 1951 and donated almost every 56 days after that! In total, he's donated 110 L (29 gal.) — enough to fill a small bathtub!

When people are injured or have surgery, they often lose blood — more blood than their bodies can replace quickly. That's where people like Dennis come in. The blood he, or anyone, donates is safely stored at a blood bank. Then when a patient needs blood, a doctor or nurse injects the donated blood into a vein of that patient to help keep her alive and healthy. Donating blood saves lives. And if the donors are healthy people older than 17, it doesn't harm them one bit.

Blood Safety

A patient who needs blood is already sick or weak, so only healthy blood will do. Before a person gives blood, a sample of it is tested to make sure it has enough iron in it.

Health-care workers also make sure the donor is not suffering from a disease that could be passed on in her blood — diseases such as malaria (muh-LARE-ee-yuh), AIDS or encephalitis (en-seff-uh-LITE-iss). And of course, the blood must be carefully labeled with its blood type. Doctors can only give someone donated blood if it is the right type to mix with the patient's without clumping.

Donated blood is usually divided into red blood cells, platelets, plasma and other components. Each of these is stored — some frozen or refrigerated — in a place called a blood bank. Plasma will keep for a year. Red blood cells can be kept for 42 days and platelets last only 5 days. Many hospitals or communities have a blood bank to keep these blood products handy.

- More than 60 million L (16 million gal.) of blood and plasma are collected each year worldwide — enough to fill more than 25 Olympic-size swimming pools.

You Try It

Don't know your blood type? If you know what blood type each of your birth parents has, you can figure out what type you DON'T have.

If your parents' blood types are:	Yours might be:	Yours definitely isn't:
A and A	A or O	B or AB
A and B	Any of A, B, AB or O	—
A and AB	A or B or AB	O
A and O	A or O	B or AB
B and B	B or O	A or AB
B and AB	A or B or AB	O
B and O	B or O	A or AB
AB and AB	A or B or AB	O
AB and O	A or B	AB or O
O and O	O	A or B or AB

If the Rh factor of both your parents is negative (−), yours will definitely be negative too. Otherwise your Rh factor could be either negative or positive. Next time you go to the doctor, ask what your blood type is. It may be written in your medical history.

Blood Maker

Your body makes blood every second of your life. In the time it takes you to read this sentence, you'll have produced about 10 million new red blood cells. Good thing too, because 10 million OLD ones died in those few seconds.

Each red blood cell lives for only about four months. Plus, you lose them other ways — when you cut yourself or get a bruise, for instance. That's why your body is constantly producing new ones. All these new blood cells come from your red bone marrow — soft, spongy tissue in the middle of the large, flat bones of your chest, your hips and your shoulder blades.

This bone marrow contains many undeveloped cells called stem cells. These can divide and grow into the millions of red blood cells you need, as well as all other types of blood cells. Large cells in the bone marrow called megakaryocytes (meg-uh-CARE-ee-oh-sites) break into pieces and become platelets.

These new cells squeeze through the thin walls of special blood vessels that run through the marrow. Then they're off into your bloodstream to get to work.

• Your body recycles! Most of the iron from your old, dying red blood cells gets reused to make new ones.

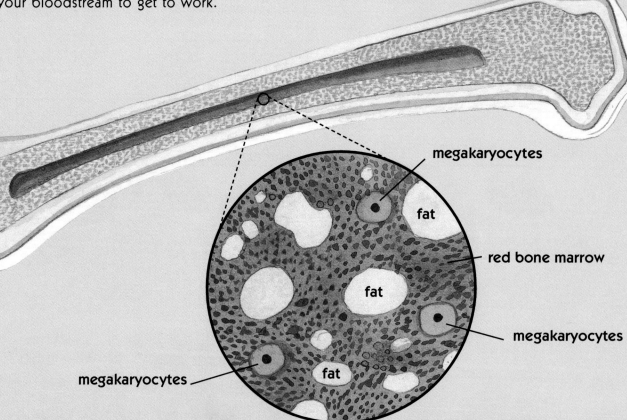

megakaryocytes

fat

red bone marrow

fat

megakaryocytes

megakaryocytes

fat

Changing Color

When you were born, you had red marrow in all of your bones. Then slowly as you got older, the red marrow in your fingers and toes changed color as yellowy fat settled into those spaces. By your fifth birthday, most of the red marrow in the long parts of your arm and leg bones had changed to yellow, too.

Once you're 25, half of your bone marrow will be red and half will have changed to yellow. Sometimes, though it's rare, a patient's yellow marrow can turn back to red and begin producing blood cells again.

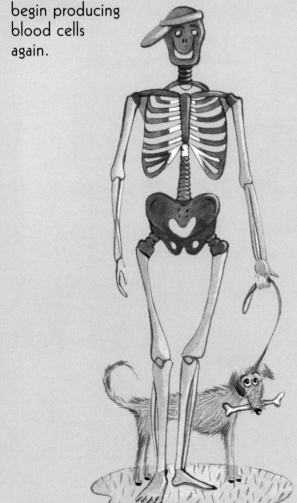

Sharing Marrow

Healthy bone marrow makes healthy new blood cells. That's exactly what people with blood-related illnesses such as leukemia (loo-KEE-me-yuh), lymphoma (lim-FO-muh) or aplastic anemia (AY-plas-tic a-NEE-me-yuh) need. So sometimes those patients get a bone-marrow transplant — marrow is taken from a healthy person and injected into the sick person. Once the marrow settles into his bones, it begins to make healthy new blood cells.

Although the marrow of the patient and donor have to match in certain ways, the two people don't have to have the same blood type. In fact, many people who get a bone-marrow transplant get a new blood type along with it.

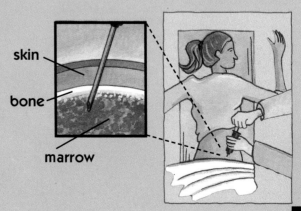

skin

bone

marrow

Bloodthirsty

When Arnold Paole moved to Medvegia, Serbia, in 1727, he talked about his adventures in Greece. The scariest one described how he'd been attacked by a VRYKOLAKAS! Vrykolakas is the Greek word for a vampire. Arnold would even show his listeners a red spot on his neck where he said the vampire had bitten him.

Arnold settled down to farming. A couple of years later, he died and was buried in the village cemetery. Within weeks, villagers began claiming they had seen him at night. About 20 of these people said Arnold had come into their homes. These same people began to get sick. Then some died. The village was in a state of panic and sent for help.

A group of soldiers and a surgeon arrived from Vienna to investigate. They opened Arnold's grave and reported that his body had not decomposed at all. He lay on his side, not on his back as he'd been buried, and his hair had grown long.

Legends from all over the world tell of vampires. Macedonians call them LAMIA. They're called LANGSUYAR in Malaysia. Legends in Nepal and Tibet tell of gods who drank blood from humans. Carvings of them show their vampire fangs. And almost everyone has heard of a vampire named Count Dracula, the main character in a famous novel.

Have there ever been real vampires? In the mid-1700s, a man named Dom Calmet documented the details of more than 700 sightings of possible vampires, including Arnold Paole, but even Calmet wasn't convinced these creatures existed.

Real Bloodsuckers

There are a few real bloodsucking creatures. Many water-dwelling leeches are haemophagic (hee-mo-FAJ-ick) parasites. That means they survive by sucking blood out of other living things nearby — fish, frogs or people.

For hundreds of years, doctors used leeches to suck what they thought was "extra" blood out of sick patients. Some leeches are still used by doctors to help get blood flowing into a hand or other limb that's been cut off in an accident and reattached by surgeons.

Female mosquitoes eat blood too, in order to produce eggs. Mosquito bites are usually harmless — unless a mosquito picks up a disease from one "victim" and passes it on to the next. Malaria, dengue (DENG-gay) fever and some types of encephalitis, including West Nile virus, are all illnesses that a mosquito could pass along.

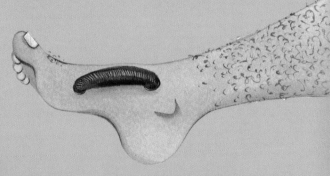

- Count Dracula is named after a real person, Vlad Dracula. This brutal ruler of Transylvania didn't drink blood, but he did have thousands of his citizens killed.

Hey!

Vampire bats of Central America don't actually suck blood. Instead they bite a cow, bird or other animal, then lick up the oozing blood. But don't worry — they almost never bite people. These bats are the only mammals that survive on blood alone. They'll die if they go two days without any.

All Pumped Up

Blood is great at carrying all the things your body needs to all the places that need it. But something has to keep the whole system moving. That's where your heart comes in.

Your heart is about the size of your fist. It sits in the upper middle part of your chest, angled slightly to the left. It's made up of four chambers — the right and left atria and the right and left ventricles. The right atrium and right ventricle work as one pump. The left ones work as another.

Blood coming in from your body travels through two large veins — the inferior vena cava (VEE-nuh CAVE-uh) and the superior vena cava — into your right atrium. The atrium gives the blood a light push into the right ventricle.

That ventricle pushes the blood hard out through your main pulmonary artery, which branches into four pulmonary arteries that carry blood to the lungs. There the blood drops off carbon dioxide it has brought from all over your body and picks up oxygen for delivery.

Your blood, now packed with oxygen, travels through the four pulmonary veins into your left atrium. One push and it's in your left ventricle, ready to be launched with the strongest push of all through your aorta (ay-OR-tuh) and other arteries out to your whole body. Then the cycle begins all over again.

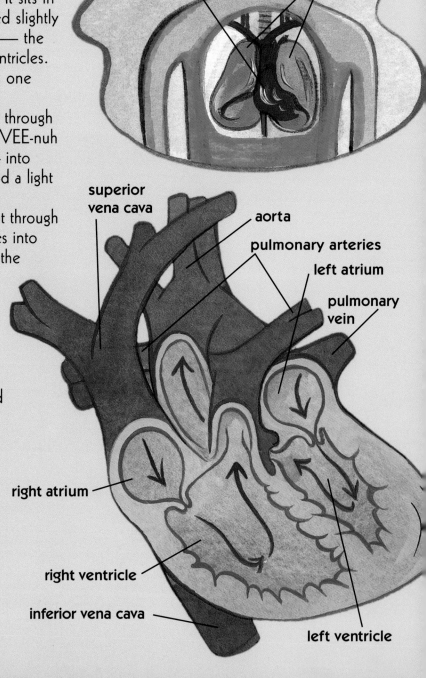

heart

lungs

superior vena cava

aorta

pulmonary arteries

left atrium

pulmonary vein

right atrium

right ventricle

inferior vena cava

left ventricle

Slamming Doors

When a doctor listens to your heart through a stethoscope, what does she hear? Doors slamming shut.

Inside your heart are four tight-fitting valves that act like doors to keep the blood from flowing back the way it came. When your atria pump blood into the ventricles, a valve between each atrium and ventricle slams shut. Then when a ventricle squeezes to pump the blood out of the heart, another valve lets the blood pass out to the arteries, then closes to keep it from slipping back into the chamber it just left.

If a heart valve is closing improperly, it makes a different sound. That's called a heart murmur. A trained doctor can recognize that sound and decide if the valve needs to be fixed.

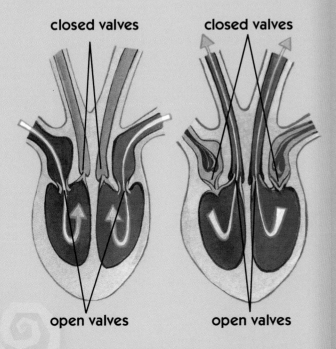

closed valves   **closed valves**

open valves   **open valves**

You Try It

Are your hands as strong as your heart? You'll need a round balloon and a measuring tape to find out.

1. Outside, fill the balloon with water. Carry it, untied, to a tall fence or wall.

2. Hold the balloon gently in both hands. Lower your hands onto the ground. Point the mouth of the balloon up and slightly toward the fence.

3. Squeeze your hands together as hard as you can to shoot a stream of water up onto the fence. Measure the height of the stream.

Your heart could send a jet of water over 2 m (6 ft.) into the air, and it does that 80 000 times every day.

The Ins and Outs of Breathing

You are like a car. A car needs oxygen to burn gas to fuel its engine, and it gives off exhaust that's left over after the fuel has burned.

Every cell in your body uses oxygen to burn fuel. The "exhaust" that's left over is carbon dioxide. Your blood brings fresh oxygen to your cells, but it also carries the waste carbon dioxide away. It's in your lungs that your blood both fills up with oxygen and drops off the waste gas.

Take a deep breath and a large muscle just below your ribs — your diaphragm (DIE-uh-fram) — pulls down, forcing oxygen-rich air to rush into your lungs — through your throat to your tubelike trachea (TRAY-kee-uh), then into the smaller and smaller passageways that branch off of it, called your bronchi (BRONG-kee) and bronchioles (BRONG-kee-olz).

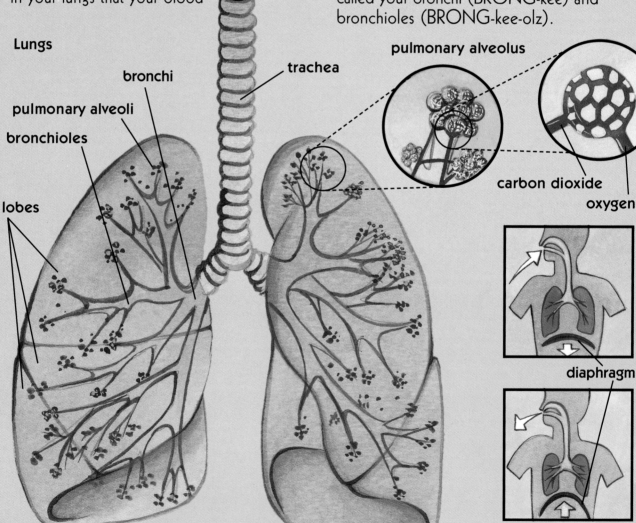

Lungs

bronchi

pulmonary alveoli

bronchioles

lobes

trachea

pulmonary alveolus

carbon dioxide

oxygen

diaphragm

A Fair Trade

At the end of each of your hair-thin bronchioles is a cluster of tiny sacs called the pulmonary alveoli (PUL-mun-air-ee al-vee-OH-lee). Each lung contains about 300 million of them. Around each alveolus are blood vessels so tiny that the blood cells have to go through them one at a time. The walls of the alveoli and these blood vessels are only 0.0005 mm (0.00002 in.) thick.

The two gases — the oxygen and the carbon dioxide — trade places by moving through the thin walls. The oxygen slips into the blood and attaches to the iron of the hemoglobin in the red blood cells. The carbon dioxide ends up in the alveoli. The buildup of carbon dioxide in your lungs and in your blood is what triggers your brain to make you breathe again.

You Try It

Find out how much air you breathe in and out with every breath. You'll need a 2 L (70 oz.) soda-pop bottle, a bendable straw, a sink and a measuring cup.

1. Fill your bottle with water and screw on the lid. Half-fill the sink with water.

2. Hold the bottle upside down with the neck under water. Reach under and remove the lid. Place one end of your straw up into the bottle.

3. Take a deep breath and blow into the straw. The air you breathe into the bottle will force out some water.

4. Still holding the bottle neck under water, screw on the lid. Lift out the bottle.

5. Measure how much water it takes to refill the bottle. That's the amount of air you breathed out.

Most people can't breathe out even half of what their lungs can hold. The lungs of an average adult hold 5 L (175 oz.), much more than a person breathes out when resting — 0.5 L (17 oz.).

Ticker Trouble

When Thomas Scott plays hockey, his efforts aren't halfhearted, even though Thomas has just half a heart.

Even before Thomas was born in 1995, doctors knew his heart had serious problems. The right ventricle was too small, there was a hole in his heart's center wall, the major arteries leading away from his heart were all in the wrong spots, and his aorta leading out to his body was very small.

All of those problems meant that Thomas's heart couldn't get enough oxygen-rich blood out to the rest of his body. So to help out his heart, doctors operated when Thomas was just three days old, again when he was eight months old and a third time just after he turned two.

Thomas's heart works now, but not in the regular way. His left ventricle, like yours, pumps blood out to deliver its oxygen and pick up carbon dioxide. From there, your blood returns to the right ventricle, which pumps it to the lungs for oxygen. Thomas's right ventricle was too small to do the job, so instead his blood goes straight to his lungs and back to his left atrium without any extra push.

As Thomas's body gets bigger, his heart may need more help circulating his blood. For right now, though, half a healthy heart is all he needs.

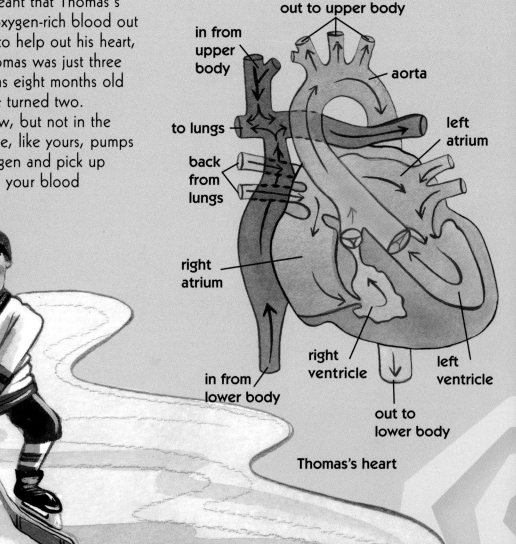

Thomas's heart

Change of Heart

In 1893, a man was brought to a Chicago hospital with a knife stuck into his heart. Dr. Daniel Hale Williams opened up the man's chest, removed the knife and stitched up the heart. He had just performed the world's first successful heart operation. Now, surgeons perform open-heart surgery regularly, even on babies, to repair or replace patients' hearts.

Babies who are born with a hole in the center wall of their heart often don't need open-heart surgery. Instead, a surgeon can insert a patch that's like a closed umbrella in through a large vein. She moves it into place, then opens it to plug the hole. Scar tissue grows around the edges and holds the patch there.

- **In the cold of the Arctic winter, the heart of the woodland frog stops beating — for weeks. The frog may seem dead, but when temperatures warm up, it hops back to life.**

Blood Supply

Your heart beats about 90 times every minute. Each beat pumps 70 mL (5 tbsp.) of blood, but your heart doesn't USE any of this blood. Instead the heart muscle gets its food and oxygen from blood that arrives through the four coronary (KOR-un-air-ee) arteries.

If any of these four gets clogged with fatty deposits, that could cause a heart attack. By exercising, eating properly and never smoking, you can help keep your coronary arteries clear. But if they do get clogged, surgeons can clear the blockages or perform bypass surgery to make new paths around them.

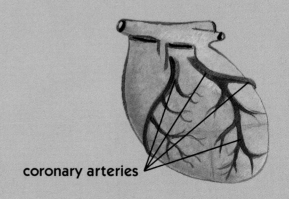

coronary arteries

Getting Around

GALEN

In A.D. 200, a doctor named Galen thought he knew how blood traveled through the body. He said that blood — which he believed was made by the liver out of food a person ate — was pumped once through the heart, from the right side to the lungs, or from the left to the rest of the body. Galen figured all this blood went out once into the body to feed it and was used up.

In 1232, a doctor known as Ibn Al-Nafis figured out that the two pumps in the heart were connected. He wrote that blood from the right side of the heart traveled to the lungs to get air, then traveled to the left side of the heart and out to the body. He was right, but his ideas were lost for hundreds of years.

It wasn't until 1628, when William Harvey, an English doctor, published his ideas that people began to realize that blood goes around and around — circulates — throughout the whole body. Harvey was the first to explain that the blood the heart pushes out through the arteries comes back to the heart through the veins.

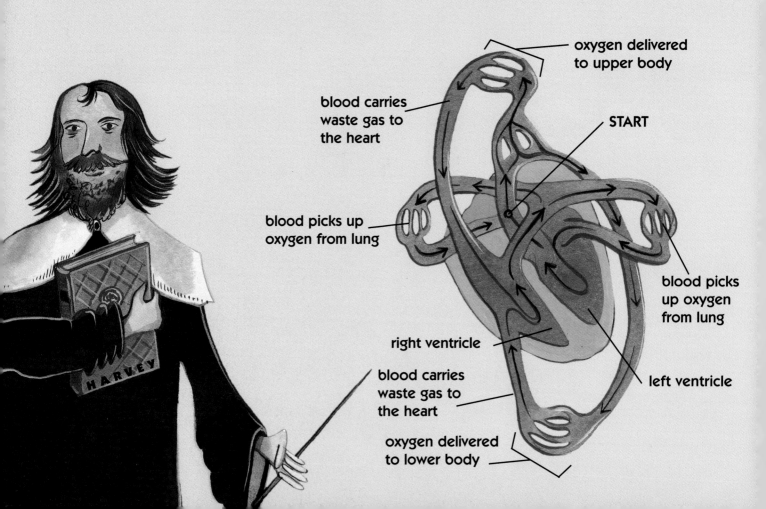

oxygen delivered to upper body

blood carries waste gas to the heart

START

blood picks up oxygen from lung

blood picks up oxygen from lung

right ventricle

left ventricle

blood carries waste gas to the heart

oxygen delivered to lower body

HARVEY

Round Trip

Time to go to school! You leap out the front door of your apartment building and run along the main streets until you get there. You go in the front door, exchange your completed homework for new assignments and leave out the back. From there, you stroll home along quiet paths leading to your back door. Inside, you head upstairs to a friend's apartment to do homework together. Then it's back to your home.

That round trip is like the one your blood takes through your body. Bright red blood chock full of oxygen leaves your heart through arteries, the busy "main street" blood vessels. It arrives at the cells in your body to drop off its oxygen and pick up wastes.

Then the blood, now a purply-red color, starts the trip back, but it takes a different route. It returns more slowly through a separate set of blood vessels — your veins. Back at your heart, the blood makes a side trip to your lungs, before heading out again and again. Every drop of blood passes through your heart about three times each minute.

- **Light bouncing off the tiny blood-filled vessels in the backs of your eyeballs is what can make your eyes look red in flash photographs.**

Connections

When is an artery almost a vein? When it's a teeny tiny capillary (CAP-ill-air-ee)! Your heart pumps blood out through big arteries, into medium-sized arteries, then into smaller and smaller ones. The tiniest vessels are thinner than a human hair. Those are capillaries. Cells can only fit through them in single file.

As blood passes through, it drops off oxygen and food to the tissues around the capillary and picks up waste carbon dioxide. The other end of each capillary is connected to tiny veins that carry the blood to larger and larger veins and finally back to the heart.

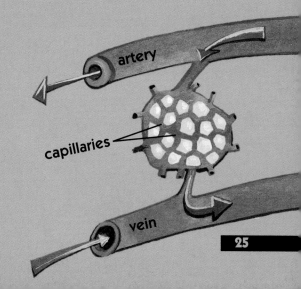

artery

capillaries

vein

Highways and Byways

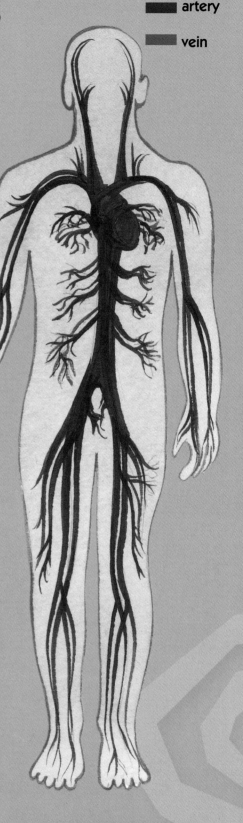

artery

vein

Your body contains a huge network of blood vessels leading to every part of your body. Some are thinner than a hair, others as thick as your thumb. By the time you're an adult, you'll have about 96 000 km (60 000 mi.) of blood vessels. If you strung them out in a single line, that line would reach right around the earth — twice!

Your heart gives your blood a strong push to send it out into your arteries. To handle those squirts of blood, arteries have walls with three layers — a smooth inner layer that blood won't stick to, a stretchy middle layer that can dilate (stretch) or constrict (tighten) depending on how much blood is there, and a strong outer layer to hold it all together.

Veins have three layers too, but their walls don't need to be so thick and stretchy. The blood they carry is much farther from the heart and doesn't have those strong pushes driving it. In fact, this blood moves so slowly that some veins contain one-way valves to keep the blood from slipping backward. The blood moves past one valve, stops, then moves to the next, like someone climbing a ladder.

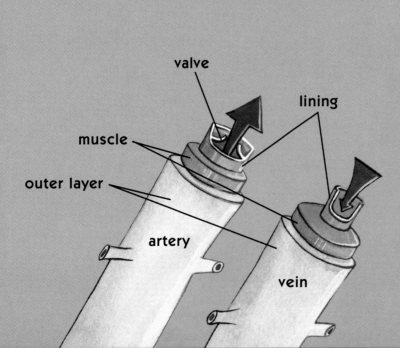

valve

lining

muscle

outer layer

artery

vein

- Mosquitoes have heat sensors to "see" where your capillaries are by the heat of the blood inside them. That's how they find the right spot to dig in.

Twisted Pathways

The valves in the veins of your legs have the tough job of keeping blood from slipping back down toward your feet. In some people, those valves weaken. Then blood on its way up to the heart instead slips down to the next valve that closes properly.

The vein gets longer in those places to hold all the extra blood, and the added length begins to look like a twisted blue tube under the skin. That's called a varicose (VARE-i-kos) vein.

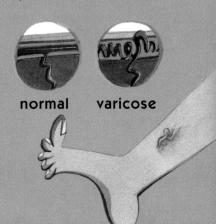

normal   **varicose**

Your lips can show you how a one-way valve in your veins works.

1. Plug your nose with your fingers.

2. Take a deep breath in, then gently close your lips.

3. Breathe out through your lips for about one second.

4. Stop breathing out and try to breathe in. What happens?

When your lips are closed, your mouth behaves a little like the one-way valves in your veins and heart. The air you breathe out forces your lips open. Air coming back the other way, however, seals the valve tightly closed and no air can get through.

Coming to the Surface

Have you ever had epistaxis (ep-i-STACK-siss)? That's what doctors call a nosebleed. The lining of your nose contains lots of tiny capillaries. Blood flowing through them brings heat from inside your body to keep your nostrils warm. That heats the air you breathe in before it travels to your lungs.

All those blood vessels are covered by only a very thin layer of tissue and the mucus (MYOO-kuss) it makes to stay moist. When the air is dry, as it is in many places in winter, the tissue dries out and cracks. Then a small bump, scratch or just the pressure of blowing your nose can make it bleed.

The best way to stop a nosebleed is to pinch your nose and push it back against your face for five minutes. That lets a clot form to seal off each broken vessel. A cold cloth or ice pack over the top of your nose helps too, since it cools the blood, making it thicken and clot faster.

Why do kids get more nosebleeds than adults? More kids pick their noses, sometimes damaging the lining.

- If you have light-colored skin, you blush when the blood vessels that carry blood to your face dilate, or widen, letting in more blood. More blood, more redness.

  How embarrassing!

Blood for Two

When you were a tiny, unborn baby, your lungs didn't work. In fact, your little heart didn't even bother pumping blood to those lungs. Instead, your mom's blood brought you all the food and oxygen you needed through arteries in the umbilical cord that connected the two of you.

Her blood also carried off your wastes when it returned to her heart and lungs through the umbilical cord's veins. Only once you were born and had to start breathing air did your lungs start working.

You Try It

In some parts of your body, your arteries are so close to the surface that you can feel the blood as your heart pumps it along.

1. Place the fingers of your left hand on the left side of your neck, just under your jaw. Can you feel a strong pulse point? That's blood flowing through your large carotid artery, on its way to your head.

2. Keep your hand on your neck while you place the fingers of your right hand on your left wrist. Feel the pulse there?

3. Sit quietly and concentrate. How does it compare to the pulse at your neck?

You should feel that the pulse at your neck is stronger and happens a split second before the pulse in your wrist. The pulse is stronger partly because the artery in your neck is larger. It's also because your neck is closer to your heart. That's why the pulse is a bit earlier. The blood gets there before it reaches your wrist.

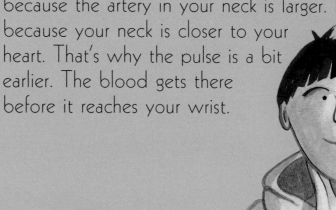

The Beat Goes On

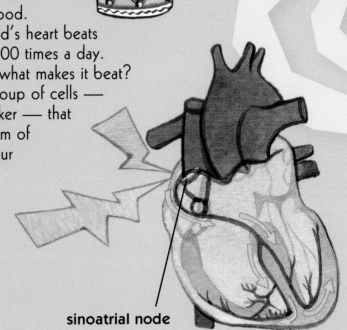

Your heart is constantly pump, pump, pumping blood. At 85 to 90 beats a minute, an average 12-year-old's heart beats more than 5000 times every hour, or about 125 000 times a day. That's nearly 44 million beats this year alone! But what makes it beat?

In the back wall of your right atrium is a small group of cells — the sinoatrial (si-no-AY-tree-yul) node, or pacemaker — that creates small pulses of electricity. The regular rhythm of electrical signals from the node is what controls your heart's beat.

The signals make the two atria contract and pump the blood they hold into the ventricles. While that's happening, the signals travel along special muscle fibers to the left and right ventricle muscles. Those contract, pumping the blood out of the heart. Then the pattern begins again.

sinoatrial node

Electric Hearts

Doctors can hook a patient up to a machine that records the electrical signals of his heart on a print-out called an electrocardiogram (ee-lek-tro-CAR-dee-oh-gram) — or ECG. That way the doctors can tell if the heart is beating regularly.

An ECG can show doctors if a heart is beating too slowly or if its beat is irregular. If so, doctors may operate to put an artificial pacemaker inside the patient's chest.

An artificial pacemaker has three main parts: a source of power, a circuit board that acts like its computer, and electrodes that

can deliver electric impulses to the heart muscle. Doctors implant the artificial pacemaker under the patient's skin in his chest. There, it keeps track of the heart's beating. If there's too long a gap between beats, the pacemaker sends an electric signal to the heart muscles to make them contract.

Restart the Heart

You've probably seen it on television: a person's heart stops, so doctors rush in and use special paddles to zap the patient's chest with electricity.

People's hearts do stop beating sometimes, especially if they've been electrocuted, badly injured or are seriously ill.

If a patient's heart stops, doctors or paramedics place their hands over her heart and do chest compressions, pushing down once or twice per second. That keeps blood flowing through her body and may get the heart restarted. Or doctors may get the heart started by injecting certain drugs.

Once the heart restarts, it may not beat in a regular rhythm. THAT'S when doctors pull out the paddles. A shot of electricity can make a heart fall back into its healthy rhythm.

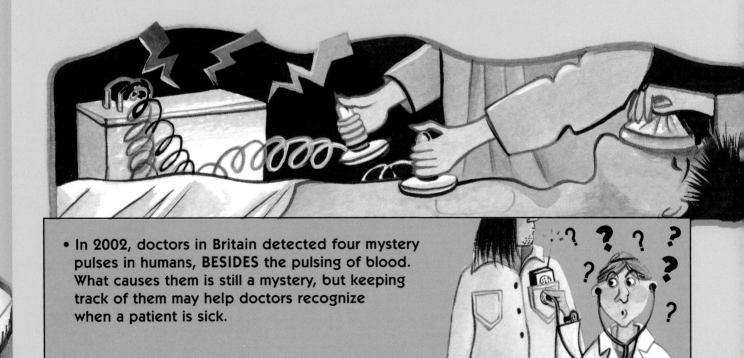

- In 2002, doctors in Britain detected four mystery pulses in humans, BESIDES the pulsing of blood. What causes them is still a mystery, but keeping track of them may help doctors recognize when a patient is sick.

Under Pressure

Has this ever happened to you? You're lying in bed j-u-s-t waking up when a voice from the kitchen calls, "The waffles are ready!" You leap to your feet — then feel dizzy and sink back onto your bed.

As you were lying there, your blood spread out evenly in your body. When you jumped up, gravity and your quick movement pulled a lot of your blood down, away from your brain. And if there's no blood pushing upward to carry oxygen to your brain, your systems begin to fail and you feel faint or dizzy. That's your body's way of making you lie down so more blood can reach your brain.

Pushing and Shoving

Your heart pushes blood into your arteries. A doctor can measure that push. It's called your blood pressure.

First, the doctor places a plastic cuff around your upper arm and pumps the cuff full of air. The pressure of that air squeezes your blood vessels and blocks the blood flow to your arm.

As the cuff slowly releases the air, blood begins to push through the blocked vessels. When it does, it makes a sound the doctor can hear through a stethoscope. Like air coming out of a balloon, blood makes the most sound when the opening is partially blocked. Once the blood is flowing through freely, there's no more sound.

The doctor watches the pressure gauge and listens to see at what pressure he can hear the blood begin to flow — that's your blood pressure during a heartbeat — and at what pressure the sounds stop — your blood pressure between beats. Those two numbers are your blood pressure. Normal blood pressure for a teenager is about 110 over 70, or 110/70. For an adult it's 120/80.

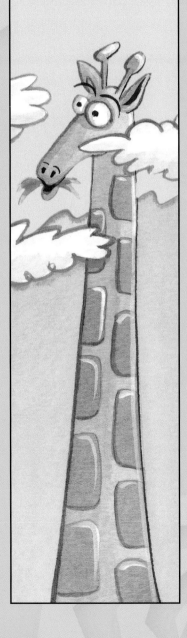

- It's a long way from a giraffe's heart to its head. Luckily, giraffes have tight skin and strong leg muscles to keep blood from settling in their legs, far from their brains.

You Try It

Astronauts wear pressure suits to keep blood from pooling in their legs during launches and landings. A thin latex glove, an elastic and some water can show you how a pressure suit works.

1. Pour water into the glove until it's half full. Seal the wrist of the glove tightly with an elastic band.

2. Lay the glove flat. The water should spread evenly through all parts of the glove, the way your blood spreads through you when you lie down.

3. Lift the glove by the wrist. What happens to the water? Mark the water level on the glove.

4. Lay the glove flat again. Gather its four fingers in one hand and hold them tightly.

5. Lift the glove by the wrist again.

A pressure suit squeezes an astronaut's legs just as you squeezed the glove's fingers. That keeps the blood closer to the heart so it can be pumped to the head.

Helping Out

Ever seen clear fluid seep out of a blister, pimple or scrape? That fluid was lymph (LIMF). It travels around your body in its own set of tubelike passages. They're part of your lymphatic (lim-FAT-ick) system.

As blood travels through you, plasma — the liquid part of blood — seeps out through the thin walls of your blood capillaries. Once it has left your blood vessels, that liquid is called lymph. Even though it's clear like water, it contains materials your cells need, including salt, nutrients absorbed from the food you eat, factors to help your blood clot and lymphocytes (LIMF-o-sites) — special white blood cells.

The lymph slips out of the capillaries, bringing the needed materials to the cells of your body. Then it seeps into tiny lymph capillaries nearby. They carry the lymph to larger lymph vessels. Eventually the lymph reaches your shoulders. There the large lymph vessels dump it back into your bloodstream through your thoracic (tho-RASS-ick) duct to begin the next circuit.

Along the way, the lymph vessels carry the lymph through bean-shaped glands called lymph nodes in your armpits, neck, groin, belly and chest. Inside these nodes, teams of white blood cells filter out harmful chemicals and germs that have gotten into your body. As they fight germs, these nodes may swell. You can sometimes feel the nodes bulging under your skin when you're sick.

> • Your tonsils and adenoids are part of your lymph system. They filter out germs in your throat to keep them out of your body.

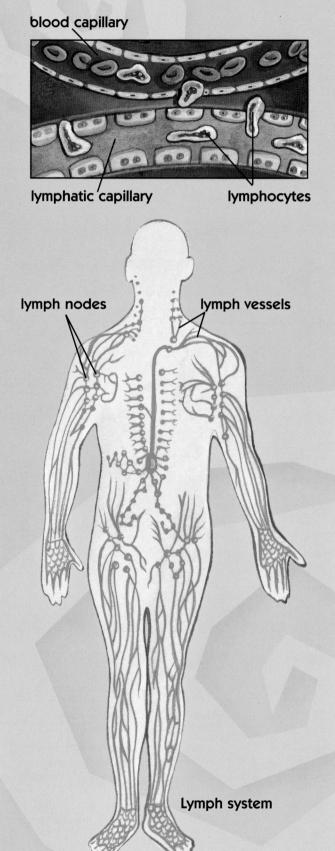

blood capillary

lymphatic capillary

lymphocytes

lymph nodes

lymph vessels

Lymph system

Your Mysterious Spleen

Your spleen is part of your lymphatic system, but doctors still aren't sure of everything that it does. It clears out old or damaged red blood cells from your blood and may filter out germs in your bloodstream like a giant lymph node. Your spleen holds extra blood, too, adding it into your bloodstream when you need it — for example, such as when you've cut yourself.

The mystery about the spleen is that it expands for about five hours after you eat. Then it slowly shrinks down again. No one yet has figured out why that happens.

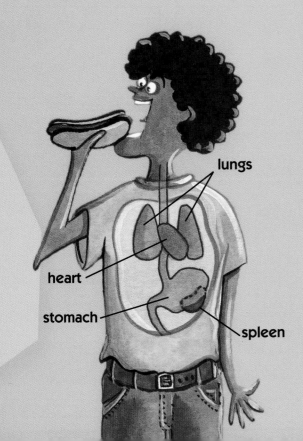

lungs

heart

stomach

spleen

Your heart pumps your blood, but there's no pump for your lymph. Instead it travels gradually through your vessels, pushed by the movement of the muscles in your body. As you walk, your leg muscles push the lymph along in that area. When you breathe, the lymph in your chest moves on.

The more the lymph moves, the more it gets filtered and added back into your blood. Some scientists think slow-moving lymph can make a person less healthy. They say exercise and massage may help get the lymph where it's going and keep you healthier.

A reptile doesn't need massage to get its lymph moving. It has a "lymph heart," usually near its tail, which pumps the lymph through its system.

The Clean Machines

Imagine what would happen if everyone in your home stopped eating one thing — bananas, maybe. If you kept buying them, they'd really start to pile up on your kitchen counter and get in the way.

Sugar in your blood can be like those bananas. Many foods that you eat — vegetables, fruits, breads — are broken down into different types of sugars. Just as bananas are food for you, the sugars are food for your cells. But if your body doesn't process them, you're in big trouble.

When sugar from digested food hits your bloodstream, your pancreas (PAN-kree-us) pumps out a hormone called insulin (IN-sull-in). Insulin triggers the cells in your body to absorb and use the sugar. The system works well as long as your pancreas is up to the job.

If someone has Type 1 diabetes (die-uh-BEE-teez), her pancreas doesn't make enough insulin. Without insulin, the cells can't absorb sugar. And too much sugar left floating in a person's blood can damage her nerves and blood vessels, especially those in the eyes, heart and kidneys. It can even lead to blindness, kidney disease or a heart attack.

People with hypoglycemia (high-poe-glie-SEE-me-uh) have the opposite problem. When they eat, their pancreas reacts to the sugar by producing too much insulin. Suddenly, the amount of sugar in their blood is too low and they feel dizzy, weak and can even go into a coma.

More Cleaners

Your pancreas isn't the only organ on clean-up duty. Your liver is like a giant filter. Every food you digest and everything you breathe in ends up in your blood. Your liver filters more than 1 L (35 oz.) of blood every minute. It removes bad stuff that finds its way into your system, such as chemicals from cigarette smoke, pesticides and — when you're old enough to drink it — alcohol.

Your two kidneys also clean your blood. They filter out wastes given off by your working muscles and wastes left over from digesting certain foods. They send those, along with any extra liquid, to your bladder so you can get rid of them the next time you visit the bathroom. Your kidneys are so good at their job, you only really need one. The second one is a backup.

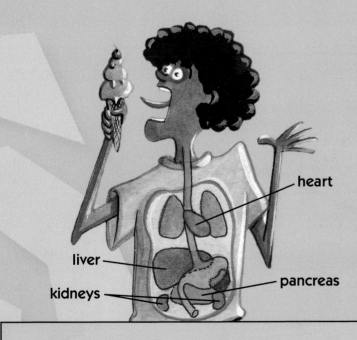

heart

liver

kidneys

pancreas

- **Except for your brain, your liver is the most complicated organ in your body.**

Type 2

There's another type of diabetes, called Type 2. The pancreas of a person with Type 2 diabetes produces insulin, but the cells don't respond to it by absorbing blood sugars. Type 2 used to mostly affect people over 40, but more and more children and teens are developing it.

Doctors think Type 2 diabetes is caused by eating too many sugary foods and not getting enough exercise. So keep active — and go easy on the soda pop and candy.

Blood of Tomorrow

Some day you may have fake blood in your veins. At least two companies are developing artificial blood they say will soon be safe for humans. One type is made using hemoglobin from red blood cells. Another is made from cow's hemoglobin that has been modified. Veterinarians have been giving one type of fake blood to dogs since 1998.

Why use fake blood? It delivers oxygen just as well as your red blood cells do, perhaps even better. More important, synthetic blood can be stored much longer than real blood, doesn't need to be refrigerated, can be given to people of any blood type and is much less likely to carry germs or disease.

One type of synthetic blood is already being given to human patients in South Africa. Not everyone agrees that these blood products are safe, though. As well, they don't last long. Real red blood cells last about 50 days — the fake hemoglobin stops working and is absorbed within 12 hours. Still, it would help patients who've lost a lot of blood. Chances are good that one day synthetic blood will be stored in every ambulance.

- If your liver stops cleaning your blood, someone else can donate part of her liver to you. Doctors now know they can give a patient part of someone else's healthy liver and both pieces will grow into full blood-filtering livers.

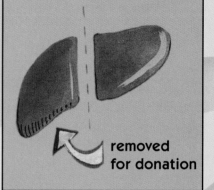

removed for donation

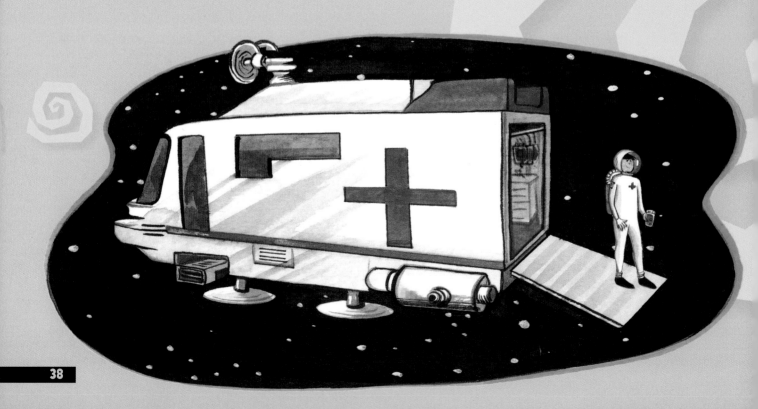

Spare Parts

Sometimes parts in a person's circulatory system break down and need fixing. Since about 1950, researchers have experimented with ways to replace heart valves that aren't working, as well as whole hearts.

Many valves made from acrylic, metal, human tissue and tissue from cows and pigs have been built over the years. Some have worked fairly well, though researchers continue to try to make one that works better.

Other researchers are working to "grow" new tissue using stem cells similar to those in your bone marrow. One company has successfully grown new blood vessels that can be implanted in a patient. Others hope to be able to grow patches of heart tissue for ailing hearts and, one day in the future, possibly even a whole heart.

But that day is probably a long way off. It's tough to copy something as amazing and complicated as your hard-working, healthy heart.

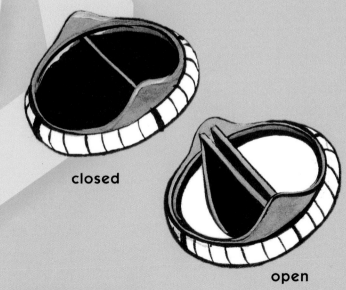

closed

open

Artificial heart valve

Plastic Pump

After 71 years of continuous pumping, Tom Christerson's heart was failing. So Tom decided to let doctors put an artificial heart inside his chest.

On September 13, 2001, Tom got his new heart, made of plastic and titanium metal. It weighed about 1 kg (2 lb.) and was connected to a small battery pack. Tom survived for 17 months, the longest anyone has ever lived with an artificial heart, before it broke down.

The human heart is a complicated muscle, but experts are hard at work to build an artificial one that will last even longer than Tom Christerson's did.

Index